G
lit

Joy

Words of encouragement and
inspiration to lift the soul

Richard Daly

Collins

Collins, a division of
HarperCollins Publishers
77–85 Fulham Palace Road

First published in Great Britain in 2008
© 2008 HarperCollins

Richard Daly asserts the moral right to be identified as the author
of this work

A catalogue record for this book is available from the British
Library

ISBN-13: 978-0-00-727837-4

1

Printed and bound in Great Britain
by Martins the Printers Ltd, Berwick upon Tweed
Typeset by MATS Typesetters, Southend-on-Sea, Essex

INTRODUCTION

Unlike other emotions, joy is a constant
state of wellbeing that does not change
with the surrounding circumstances
of life that often influence our feelings.
Joy is an inner confidence, knowing that
God is there and there is nothing to fear
for the future. It is also an acknowledgement
of being the recipient of the present
blessings from Him.

This little book is designed to help you
to be in tune with this source of joy and to
challenge you to step out in faith that
you will begin to see the fruits of living
a life free from the cares and worries
of this world.

CLAIM YOUR JOY

It is God's every desire that your
life be filled with joy. To you He says,
'May your joy be full.'

John 15:11

BELIEVE IN YOURSELF

Look in the mirror. Go ahead, face yourself and announce, 'I'm full of untapped potential.'

Philippians 2:13

GET INFECTED

'Joy is very infectious...be always
full of joy.'

Mother Teresa

Mathew 10:8

JOY FOR KEEPS

When God gives you joy,
no-one can take it from you.

John 16:22

FINISH YOUR TO DO LIST

Set reasonable goals so that by the
end of the week you can complete your
tasks. When Friday comes feel the
weight of worry lift off your shoulders.

Genesis 2:1-2

SHOUT TO THE LORD

Whether or not you can sing, you can 'make a joyful noise unto the Lord.'

Psalm 100

OPEN THE DOOR

God knows how to turn things around.
He can turn your sorrow into
joy – just let Him in.

Psalm 41:22
Jeremiah 31:13

RENEW YOUR JOY DAILY

The reason God blesses you
every day is simply because He wants you
to be joyful every day.

Ecclesiastes 7:14

A STEADFAST JOY

To be joyful is a principle. It doesn't change
with emotions. Joy is an inner contentment
despite all the circumstances.

Ecclesiastes 2:10
Ezra 6:22

GET POWER THROUGH JOY

The scriptures declare 'the joy
of the Lord is your strength.'

Nehemiah 8:10

WAIT FOR THE HARVEST

'They that sow in tears
shall reap in joy.'

Psalm 126:5

SEEK GOD'S WILL

Make sure that what you want is
what God wants for you! Then your joy
will be complete.

Ephesians 5:16-17

RISE ABOVE YOURSELF

Mediocrity is just the best
of the worst and the worst of the
best. Is that what you want? No? Then
get out of your comfort zone!

Ecclesiastes 9:10

LET GOD FIX IT

If God's dealing with greed, lust, pride or
any other obstacle in your path – don't get in
His way!

John 3:6

LET GOD FINISH

To be joyful...try less and trust more. The
Bible says 'He who began a good work
in you will carry it onto completion.'

Philippians 1:6

BE GRATEFUL

When you consider that God
knows all about your sin, yet
promises to offer forgiveness, it ought to give
you a heart of thankfulness

Daniel 9:10

FORGIVE JOYFULLY

Real forgiveness is a lifelong
commitment. You must practice it
everyday. It's not easy, but the rewards
abound in joy.

2 Corinthians 2:7
Luke 6:37

MAKE THE RIGHT CHOICE

'You can think and act yourself
into dullness or unhappiness. By the same
process you can build up inspiration
and a surging depth of joy.'

Norman Vincent Peale

Deuteronomy 30:19-20

EMBRACE GOD'S LOVE

God's love will heal your
emotions, raise your self-esteem
and put a foundation of self-worth
and joy within you. Embrace that love today.

Romans 8:31-39

REST UP

Your joy can easily be robbed when you
allow yourself to become emotionally and
physically drained. Reclaim your joy
by seeking tranquillity.

Isaiah 30:15

ORDER YOUR PRIORITIES

To live a life with joy is more
rewarding than a 'successful' life without it.

Job 20:5

LOOK FOR JOYFUL SIGNS

You will know when you are joyful in the
Lord; it leads to the feelings of praise,
thankfulness, worship
and adoration of God.

Psalm 34:1

TASTE THE FRUITS

The Fruits of the Spirit are love, joy,
peace, patience, kindness, goodness,
faithfulness, humility and self-control.

Galatians 5:22

SERVE JOYFULLY

Acts of service always lead
to scenes of joy.

1 Corinthians 13:4

THE WORD OF LIFE

The words in the Bible contain so much life
and power. They're stronger than any therapy.
God can give you a word that goes back into your
past, and heal your yesterday, secure your today
and anchor your tomorrow. Start
tapping into that power today.

Ephesians 3:20

APPRECIATE GOOD IN OTHERS

It takes more than one colour to
make a rainbow. When you learn to
appreciate the difference in people, you
will find it all contributes to the whole picture.

Philippians 2:2-3

DO IT 100%

Be absolutely determined to
enjoy what you do.

1 Corinthians 10:31

GIVE YOURSELF BACK TO GOD

Consider your life as a gift
from the Creator. Your gift back
is letting him fill it with joy.

Luke 6:38

PASS JOY ON

To have joy is to share it.

2 Corinthians 9:7
Acts 20:35

WORK, REST AND PLAY

Live and work but don't forget to
play, have fun in life and really
enjoy it.

Philippians 2:2

SAFEGUARD YOUR JOY

Don't let anyone steal your joy!

Revelation 3:11

SEEK JOY FROM GOD

Remember, joy never came from riches or wealth
or the praise of men. Such a belief will
always be a myth.

Acts 8:20
1 Timothy 6:10

BE A BLESSING

Since you get more joy out of
giving to others, put a lot more thought
and effort into the happiness you are able to give.

Romans 12:14

CULTIVATE JOY

'The greater part of our joy or misery
depends on our dispositions and not on
our circumstances. We carry the seeds of
one or the other in our minds wherever we go.'

Martha Washington

Psalm 126:6

DON'T SETTLE
FOR HALF MEASURES

Jesus said 'These things have I spoken to
you that my joy might remain in
you and that your joy might
be full.'

John 15:11-12

SACRIFICIAL GIVING

'There is a wonderful law of
nature that the three things we crave most
in life – joy, freedom and peace of mind –
are always attained by giving them to
someone else.'

Helen Keller

Matthew 25:35-40

ENJOY YOURSELF!

It's a misconception to believe that having
fun can't be God's will. The God who
made giraffes, a puppy's tail, a young girl's
giggle – has a sense of humour. Make no
mistake about that!

Psalm 37:4

THE TIME IS NOW

If you are unable to experience joy in
this season of your life, what other
season shall you wait for?

2 Kings 7:9

CHOOSE LASTING JOY

The difference between shallow happiness and
a deep joy is sorrow. When sorrow arrives
happiness dies. It can't stand
pain. Joy, on the other hand, rises from
sorrow and therefore withstands all grief.

Job 41:22
Psalm 51:11

TRUST IN GOD

Joy is the deep seated confidence
that God is in control of every
area of your life.

Proverbs 3:5-6.

STOP COMPLAINING

'The happiest people don't worry
too much about whether life is
fair or not, they just get on
with it.'

Andrew Matthews

Proverbs 16:20
John 6:43
Philippians 2:14

FIND JOY THROUGH TRIALS

The things we try to avoid and
fight against – tribulation, suffering and
persecution – are the very things that produce
abundant joy in us.

Romans 8:37
2 Corinthians 7:4

TRUST GOD'S TIMING

'Our Heavenly Father never takes anything from His children unless He means to give them something better.'

George Muller

Luke 11:10-13.

FOLLOW CHRIST'S EXAMPLE

The joy Jesus experienced came from
doing what His father sent him to do. He says to
us, 'As the father sent me, so send I you.'

John 20:21

BE TRANSFORMED

'God not only takes away the
bitterness in your life and gives sweetness
in its place, but turns the bitterness
into something itself.'

Charles Spurgeon

Jeremiah 13:13

EXPERIENCE HEALING JOY

The experience of joy has many healing wonders,
it strengthens your immune system, burns away
impurities, shapes your intellect, dispenses
worries and other negative emotions.

Isaiah 35:10

LIFT HIM UP!

'Rejoice in the Lord always;
again I say rejoice.'

Philippians 4:4.

BE CHILDLIKE

Children smile 400 hundred times a day on
average...adults 15 times.
Children laugh 150 times a day...adults 6 times.
Children play 4 – 6 hours a day...adults
only 20 minutes
What has happened?

Ecclesiastes 12:1-7

THE JOY IN YOU

Joy has nothing to do with material things.
A person living in luxury can be wretched, yet a
person in the depths of poverty,
overflowing with joy.
Joy's not in things, it's in you!

Proverbs 23:7
Luke 6:45.

GET INTO PERSPECTIVE

'In the end it's not the years
in your life that count. It's the
life in your years.'

Abraham Lincoln

John 10:10

THE FUTURE'S BRIGHT

'A pessimist sees the difficulty in
every opportunity; an optimist sees the
opportunity in every difficulty.'

Winston Churchill

Psalm 71:14
Lamentations 3:26

CLAIM YOUR GIFT

'Yesterday is history, tomorrow is a mystery
and today is a gift; that's why they
call it the present.'

Anon

James 1:17
2 Kings 7:9

JOYFUL IN SADNESS

We can be joyful and happy at
the same time, but more importantly,
when life's circumstances deal us a hard blow
we can be joyful though unhappy.

Psalm 35:9
2 Corinthians 7:4

REVEL IN SIMPLICITY

Buy a single rose, tulip or daisy. Admire
the smell, colour and shape of the petals and
remember how beautiful life can be.

Genesis 1:31
Psalm 104:24

JUMP FOR JOY

Literally. Hopping up and down in places for
30 seconds infuses you with energy and
youthful vigour.

John 3:2

MEDITATE WHILE YOU WALK

Stroll through a familiar part of town
and focus your mind on sights,
smells and sounds.

Psalm 8:3

REMEMBER KIND ACTS

Recall a situation in which a friend
treated you kindly. Mentally extend
the feelings of joy that inspired you.

2 Peter 1:7-8

DO THE TWIST

This dance style is fun, silly and easy
and it will make you laugh.

Psalm 30:11
Ecclesiastes 3:4

CREATE AMBIANCE

For tonight's dinner, put out your best
tablecloth, create a centrepiece, or simply light
a candle. A festive setting makes
for a festive mood.

2 Timothy 6:17

GET OUTSIDE

Whenever you feel bored or gloomy, go
for a walk. The fresh air, changing scenery
and exercise will boost your mood.

Psalm 121:1

TAKE LESSONS

It's not too late to learn a hobby…like knitting,
playing the piano, horse riding…hobbies are
fun and release stress.

Ecclesiastes 2:10

LOOK TO THE HEAVENS

Whenever possible,
relax under the stars. Gazing at the
night sky makes you feel more
connected to the world.

Job 22:12
Romans 1:21

STAY CONNECTED

Jesus says 'I am the vine, you are
the branches.' You are not blessed in any
endeavour because of your performance, you're
blessed because of your connection to the vine.

John 15:5

FORGIVE IT AND DROP IT

You cannot really forgive without
the Holy Spirit's help. None of us can. So
today why don't you pray, 'Holy Spirit,
breathe on me and give me the strength
to forgive _____ for
what they did. Heal me of my wounds...'

Mark 11:25

INTERCEDE

Prayer isn't just about you. It's about others.
Your prayer moves God. God moves people.
People bring about change. The whole thing
begins with one praying person – today
let that person be you.

Psalm 106:23

A JOY THAT TRANSFORMS

If you're tired of the way your
life's going and don't like what
you're becoming, pray
the Psalmist David's prayer
in Psalm 51: 'Create in me a clean
heart and renew in me a right spirit.'

Psalm 51

ACCEPT GOD'S WORD

God's promises NEVER FAIL...Every one of them
are like precious jewels just waiting
to be discovered.

2 Peter 3:9
2 Corinthians 1:20

CLAIM GOD'S PROMISES

Because your God is a covenant-
making, covenant-keeping God, what he
has spoken over your life He will surely
bring it to pass. Depend on it.
God keeps His word.

Romans 3:4

BE JOYFUL IN PATIENCE

No matter how long it takes, wait
for God's timing. He always shows
up at the right time.

Isaiah 40:31
Lamentations 3:26

LET GO OF HATRED

Endeavour to forgive those who have done you
wrong, just as Christ has forgiven you.
Bitterness is fatal. It kills your joy.

Colossians 3:13

CONFESS AND FORSAKE

'Confession is good for the soul.' It cleanses and
purges you from guilt and shame and allows the
Spirit of Jesus to surface once again.

Proverbs 28:13
1 John 1:9

DETERMINE YOUR PRIORITIES

If you're too busy to reach out
to those who are hurting, you're just too busy!

Luke 10:33

START AFRESH TODAY

You can't do anything about your past,
but starting right now you can change
your future – one choice and one
act at a time.

Matthew 16:27

HEAVENWARD BOUND

Many of the rewards God has for
you are so great it'll take eternity to
appreciate and enjoy them. That's why He
wants you in heaven!

Luke 14:14
John 14:1-3

JUDGE NOT

When God wants to bless you, sometimes
He'll send a person – your boss, the tax man, the
mortgage lender, the post man or even those
who mean you no good!

Philippians 4:19

TRUST GOD'S FAITHFULNESS

When you appreciate God's blessings you will be
able to say in difficult times, 'If He blessed me
before, He'll do it again' – and press on.

Hebrews 13:8
Malachi 3:6

STEP UP

When God is on your side, obstacles
become opportunities for growth!

Philippians 3:13-14

LET GO

Waiting is difficult but it serves a
vital purpose. Above all else it means
making a daily decision to trust and obey God
even when things are not going
the way you planned.

Hebrews 6:15

GET CLEAN

When you accept Christ, He changes
you from the inside out.

2 Corinthians 5:17

IN HEAVEN'S EYES

Through prayer you get to know
God's heart and start seeing yourself through
His eyes. When that happens you'll never see
yourself in the same way again!

Isaiah 55:8
1 Corinthians 13:12

DON'T LOSE HEART

Regardless of your circumstances, keep
your joy alive today by staying
focussed on God!

Job 11:18

SEE THE GOOD

Being joyful is letting those we love
be perfectly themselves, not twisting them
to fit our own image. Otherwise our joy will
only be based on the reflection of ourselves
that we see in them.

Colossians 3:13

BE AMAZED BY GRACE

No matter what you've done or how
far you've fallen, you can receive
God's love and joy and mercy. It's called grace.

Ephesians 2:5
2 Corinthians 12:9

AN AWESOME GOD

Jesus is the only man ever to make an
appointment beyond the grave and show up for it!
That's the kind of God you serve!

John 11:25

KEEP THE COMMANDMENTS

When asked to identify what the
law was about, Christ simply replied
'Love God and love people.' This is the
foundation of joy.

1 John 4:8

CHECK YOUR ATTITUDE

Mother Teresa always worked with a joyful
attitude. If somebody could be joyful
amongst the dying and the
poorest of the poor, surely you can too!

Isaiah 61:10

KEEP ON PRAISING

To maintain a joyful attitude the
Psalmist said, 'seven times
a day I praise you' – try it.

Psalm 119:164

GET YOURSELF RECYCLED

Christ loves to salvage and recycle the
hurting, the throw-aways, the left-overs,
the used-ups and the put-downs,
and fill them with joy.

Luke 19:10

PRACTISE WHAT YOU PREACH

Your Bible knowledge may be 10 times
greater than someone else's, but
if you're not 10 times more loving, patient
and joyful, what good is it?

Deuteronomy 11:18

TIME FOR A SCRUB

God's word is the only
detergent strong enough to get down into the
deepest levels of our thoughts, imagination and
motives and cleanse us.

Hebrews 4:12

PASS IT ON

You're blessed to be a blessing.

Genesis 12:2

OPEN THE DOOR

'If you want joy, real joy, wonderful
joy...let Jesus come into your heart.'

Proverbs 23:26
Revelation 3:20

THE REASON FOR THE SEASON

'Joy to the world. The Lord has come.'
This favourite carol reflects the true
reason why we can have joy today.

Matthew 1:21

LIVE TO GIVE

There is tremendous joy in giving.
It is a very important part of
the joy of living.

Matthew 10:8

DON'T WASTE TIME

Time is fleeting. Often a second chance
never comes. Don't hesitate
to do something good – a
note of appreciation, a card of thanks,
a word of gratitude.

John 9:4
Matthew 25:13
Proverbs 27:1

A NEW HOPE

Today is a new day...a fresh start.

Lamentations 3:23

BE PROACTIVE

Refuse to spend time worrying about
what might happen. Determine to spend time
making things happen.

1 Corinthians 3:14
2 Thessalonians 1:11

LET JOY RADIATE FROM YOU

Joyful people are more likely to be
confident, positive in thinking, healthy and have
attractive personalities. It certainly pays off!

Proverbs 15:13

WATCH OUT FOR COMPLACENCY

Constantly thank God for the things we
often take for granted...sight, sound, touch, taste,
hearing...and loved ones!

Songs of Solomon 8:7

THE BEST MEDICINE

Laughter is 'to express emotion or amusement by
expelling air from the lungs in short
bursts to produce an inarticulate voiced
noise.' All you need is something to
trigger it off!

Ecclesiastes 3:4

KEEP JOY ALIVE

If joy is strength, its absence
creates weakness.

Nehemiah 8:10

JUST DO IT

If we wait until conditions are
perfect, it will never happen.
If we are going to rejoice,
find a reason today.

Psalm 68:3
Psalm 118:24

CAST YOUR BURDENS

Worry makes us depend on ourselves,
it robs us of joy and energy.

Proverbs 24:19

CHOSEN

With full knowledge of your
past failings and present defects of
character, God chose you anyway. That
is mind-blowing grace!

John 15:16

CHECK YOUR MOTIVES

If you feel unrecognised and
unrewarded for what you do, ask yourself
who am I doing it for?

1 Corinthians 10:31

NURTURE JOY

While God has given us the
capacity for joy, we must make every
effort to develop that joy, release it,
and walk in it at all times.

2 Timothy 1:6

PUT OTHERS FIRST

Only when we decide to
practise sacrificial love and put away the
old 'me-first' lifestyle, will the joy
and power of God's love be released through
our lives.

Ephesians 5:2

REFLECT YOUR JOY

The most readily identifiable
outward characteristic of the Christian is
joy. If something has happened inside, it ought to
show on the outside!

Matthew 5:16

MINUS TO PLUS

The Psalmist said 'It was good
for me to be afflicted so that I might
learn your decrees.' God loves to turn our
negatives into positives.

Psalm 119:71

FIND JOY WITHIN

'Joy is not in things, it is in us.'

Richard Wagner

Isaiah 30:29
Matthew 5:8

THANKS FOR EVERYTHING

Paul writes 'In everything give thanks...'
In uncertainty give thanks,
in heartache give thanks.
In poverty and in prosperity give thanks.

1 Thessalonians 5:18

BE IN CONTROL

When you can laugh in spite of
your circumstances, it shows that
temporal situations don't control your joy.

Philippians 2:17-18
Proverbs 17:22

BE AN ENCOURAGER

We all need encouragement and
the beautiful thing about encouraging
is that anybody can do it.

1 Thessalonians 5:11

STICK AT IT

Jesus said 'You will weep and
mourn...but eventually your grief
will turn to joy...and no one
will take it away.'

Luke 16:20-22

BE DIVINELY PROTECTED

If we saw the snares Satan
lays for us...how we would adore
the Lord who enables
us to escape them all!

Psalm 103:2

A NEW LEASE OF LIFE

The Psalmist said 'The Lord…redeems
your life from destruction.' When others
write you off, He signs you up.

Psalm 103:2

BE YOUR OWN AUTHOR

Your life is a story. Each day
you get to write a new page. So,
fill those pages with joyful moments. When
you look back you won't be disappointed.

2 Timothy 4:7

SPEND PRECIOUS MOMENTS

Spend quality time with those people
in your life to whom you're irreplaceable.

Psalm 90:12

DON'T WASTE TIME

Time is an equal-opportunity employer.
We all get 24 hours / 1,440 minutes / 86,400
seconds daily and we must account for how
we use them.

Romans 14:2

LET JOY FLOW

When you bless others, you open up your
heart as a channel for God to bless you.

Acts 20:35
Ephesians 6:8

BE SATISFIED

Be careful for the love of 'more.'
You risk losing appreciation of your
God-given blessings.

Hebrews 13:5

SEEK CONTENTMENT

The apostle Paul says,
'I have learned in whatever
state I am, to be content.' That's something
to strive for!

Philippians 4:11
Proverbs 15:16

JUST BE SATISFIED

Pursue the virtue of contentment, for
'Godliness with contentment
is great gain.'

1 Timothy 6:6

LET GOD RESHAPE YOU

God doesn't waste anything. He uses
all our experiences – the good, the bad, and
the ugly – to prepare us.

Philippians 3:21

WAIT FOR THE REASON

If you're struggling to see God's
purpose in your suffering today, rest
assured He has one. When you trust Him,
He makes 'all things work together for good.'

Romans 8:28

LOVE GOD, LOVE OTHERS

Contentment and fulfilment are
achieved when we walk straight along the path
the Lord has set before us.

Psalm 119:105
Mathew 19:17

EXPERIENCE JOY IN DOING

'Do all the good you can, by all the means
you can, in all the places you can at all the
times you can to all the people you can,
as long as you ever can.'

John Wesley

Zechariah 4:10

STAYING POWER

God doesn't just strengthen you once…He'll
strengthen you again and again
as and when the need arises.

Ephesians 6:13

JOYOUS IN WAITING

Just because it hasn't happened yet
doesn't mean God has changed His mind. While
you are waiting, God is working.

James 1:4

JOYFULLY ASSURED

You can start thanking God
today for what He will do for you tomorrow,
because He will, absolutely will,
come through for you!

Isaiah 65:24

BE JOYFUL IN PRAYER

Our goal in prayer should be to
maintain such a close relationship with God
that we can communicate back and forth
no matter what the time of day or situation.

Ephesians 3:12

WORRY KILLS JOY

If we really believe that God cares
for us – we won't need to worry
about worrying things.

Psalm 23:4
Matthew 8:26

TAKE IT OR LEAVE IT

Joy is not something that comes in different levels,
portions or sizes – you either have it, or you don't.

John 16:24

BE AN OPEN CHANNEL

Like the Dead Sea, God never intended us
to be reservoirs that just take in. He
called us to be rivers that flow out
to bless others.

Proverbs 11:24-25
2 Corinthians 9:7-8
Ecclesiastes 11:1-2

SOW JOYFUL SEEDS

Even if you don't have a specific need
right now, sow a seed of kindness…you never
know who might reap it in the future.

Psalm 126:5
Hosea 10:12

LOVE IN ACTION

Loving God is an
attitude resulting in action. It's a daily decision to
acknowledge Him in all that you say and do.

Revelation 2:4
1 Corinthians 13:7-8

BEING LOVED LEADS TO JOY

Sometimes our actions make us unlovely
but we are never unloved.
Because God loves us we are valued.
Enjoy that thought.

1 John 3:1

PLANS TO PROSPER YOU

How do you know if God still
has a plan for you? Because you are
still breathing! His
plans never expire.

Jeremiah 29:11

PRACTISE WHAT YOU PREACH

How much of the advice you
give to others do you actually practise
yourself? Living what you believe to
be true is a sure path to joyful living.

Mark 4:14
Colossians 3:17
James 1:22

DON'T LOSE YOUR TEMPER

Next time you get all worked up ask
yourself, 'What is the enemy trying to do
here?' Be sure, ultimately he wants
to steal your joy!

Ephesians 4:27

LOVE YOURSELF AGAIN

Times of despondency, despair and depression can
often remove feelings of self-worth and
love. It's during the time of darkness that God's
light seeks to shine brighter
reminding you that you are precious.

Psalm 139:17
Jeremiah 31:3

HAPPY ARE THE JOYFUL

Joy is more than what we
call happiness. Joy is the enjoyment
of God and the good things that come from Him.

Psalm 16:11
Romans 14:17

FILL UP CONTINUALLY

Joy is the fuel God injects our life
to run on.

Romans 15:13

NEW DAY, NEW BEGINNINGS

Welcome each new morning
with a smile on your face, love in your
heart and good thoughts on your mind.

Psalm 63:5
Isaiah 61:10

CHERISH THE GIFT

This day with its blessings and
challenges is a gift from God, so don't
insult Him by complaining.

Philippians 2:14

GROW OLD GRACIOUSLY

A life of gratitude and service will keep
you young until you die. A life of complaining
will age you prematurely. Stop your
complaining!

Ephesians 5:20
1Timothy 4:3
Psalm 26:7

TAKE CONTROL

To get up each morning with the
resolve to be happy...is to set our
own conditions to the events of the day.
To do this is to condition circumstances
instead of being controlled by them.

Ralph Emerson
1 Corinthians 1:17-18

OBEY THE COMMANDER

'Rejoice in the Lord always!'
Joy is a command. It's non-optional
and non-negotiable.

Deuteronomy 28:8
Psalm 42:8

BOUGHT WITH A PRICE

Just think: the God of the universe
willingly left the splendour of heaven,
was born into poverty and died for
wayward humanity. Why?
That we may have abundant joy in Him!

Philippians 2:7

BE SHAPED BY THE POTTER

You may be 'flawed' and 'limited' but
the God who lives and works in you is not!

Philippians 2:13

DISCOVER YOUR GIFTS

Often the qualities we see in other
people are already available within you.
Cultivate your God-given gifts
and appreciate them.

2 Corinthians 4:7

THE BLESSED HOPE

In order to keep us from
becoming too attached to this world, God
reminds us of its ugliness – to keep
our hearts longing for a better world.

John 14:1-3
1 Peter 1:17

PERSONALISE YOUR JOY

Repeat this sentence by filling
in the blank with your name:
God loves _____ so much that He died
so that _____ can experience God's
joy in his / her life today!

Mark 9:23
John 1:7
John 11:40

SMALL GIFTS

Life's most rewarding experiences
rarely come in neat little packages.
They're often found in little unexpected
encounters. Watch out for them!

Luke 10:31-32.

JUST ASK

If you want joy in your life
then sincerely ask God for it. It's that simple!
He's waiting to bestow it within you today!

Matthew 7:7-8